July 2 '09

a gift for
BIG MOSHI
KESIA

from
LI'L MOSHI
MARIA

I am grateful
for friends like
you! Happy Birthday!
JI

Editorial Director: Todd Hafer
Editor: Jeff Morgan
Art Director: Kevin Swanson
Designer: Michelle Nicolier
Lettering Artist: Calvert Guthrie
Production Artist: Dan Horton

ISBN: 978-1-59530-169-7
BOK5519

Printed and bound in China.

good things great and small

a whole lot of reasons to be thankful

GIFT BOOKS
from Hallmark

When daily life sometimes seems plagued with small aggravations and annoyances,

it's good to realize that it is also filled with blessings. If we make an effort to look and listen, we might be surprised at how much there is to be thankful for—a common but favorite snack, an old familiar melody, the love of family, a particular shade of blue, pleasant memories, a child's exuberant laugh, a pet's devotion, an unexpected courtesy, a distant birdsong. The list could go on and on—and in the following pages it does. Join with the Hallmark writers who contributed to them in realizing just how many things, big and little, we all have to be thankful for at any given moment. So read on and smile…and feel better about whatever kind of day it is.

Smiles

I'M GRATEFUL FOR smiles from strangers. I live in a friendly city, so it's not like people brush past each other in a purposeful rush, but there's a certain unexpected warmth that some people send out when I least expect it. Sometimes the friendly person is young and fashionable, and that makes me think, hey—it is cool to be friendly. And sometimes if the smiler isn't necessarily young, great-looking, or on top of the world, I realize that if that person has goodwill enough to spare, I can let my inner smiley person show, too.

Ellen Brenneman

THANK HEAVENS FOR wagging tails.
I love them. The long, the stubby,
the straight, the curly, the furry…
the happy, crazy, round-the-world wag,
the twirling-in-circles-while-wagging wag.
All of them. Every one. Every time.
Because no matter what is screwed
up in my world, a wagging tail is always,
unequivocally a very good thing.

Jeannie Hund

wagging tails

HOW I KNOW LIFE IS GOOD:

My teenagers say "love you"
on their way out the door.

My big black Lab thumps her tail on the floor
when I come downstairs in the morning.

I can depend on my friends
for at least one good belly laugh a day.

After 24 years, my husband and I
still get a kick out of each other.

I never again will have to suit up
and climb a rope. Or go to summer camp.

Macaroni and cheese. Mmmm.
Macaroni and cheese.

Molly Wigand

I AM GRATEFUL FOR
the freedom to travel,
to speak my mind,
to read what I want,
and to vote for change.

Carolyn Hoppe

I'M NOT JUST GRATEFUL for music—I couldn't live without it. Or I could, but why bother? Never to hear a new song or sing along with an old one. Never to crank up the stereo or plunk down at the piano. No memories stuck to Beatles' songs. No goose bumps at the beginning of Barber's *Adagio for Strings* or tears at the end. Never to put on *Kind of Blue* late at night and let Miles tell my life story. Without music, that story would be the blues, with no blues to make it worth hearing.

Jim Howard

I'M GRATEFUL THAT time heals all wounds, especially when you're talking about the pain of a really bad haircut.

Dierdra Zollar

I'M GRATEFUL FOR mothers
who still call and check
on their children,
no matter how old they are—
and still know just what to say
to make things better.

Kamilah Aisha Moon

THINGS I LOVE

Cool sheets on a warm night
Sunshine in January
Autumn leaves
Tuna melts
Back-to-school supplies
Fresh peaches

Love letters

Beverly Laudie

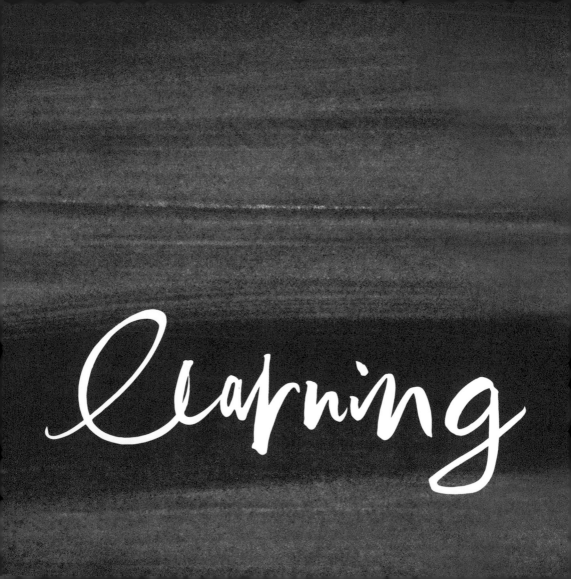

WHAT A BRILLIANT idea—adult education classes. Want to learn to belly dance? There's nothing stopping you. Scriptwriting? Just sign up. Have a hidden desire to trip the light fantastic? Take a class. From throwing pots to throwing karate punches, there are opportunities to stretch and grow and find out what you're made of.

Lisa Riggin

I'M GRATEFUL FOR
hot cheesy goodness.
On anything. Pizza,
sandwiches, pasta,
potatoes, on crackers,
in dips, and just all by itself.
Hot cheesy goodness.
Also, I'm grateful for
stretch denim.

Melvina Young

I'M GRATEFUL FOR the lazy sunlight in my living room on a Sunday afternoon. For the pillow propped beside the arm of a couch and the book I can't put down. For a fresh glass of water, a cat purring on my belly, and the gradual feeling of sleepiness stealing across my eyelids. For the blanket I pull across me and for that feeling of having nothing to do for a few hours, so I'm fine to sleep, right where I am, until whenever I wake up.

Lauren Benson

a Sunday

afternoon

MY DAD USED TO PLAY a game with me, my brother, and my sister that he called "Tackle on the Five." It was a pretty simple game—he'd get on his knees on the living room floor, we'd run at him trying to get past, and he'd try to tackle us. I wanted to get tackled, because the tackle was a lift-you-in-the-air tickle-tackle that brought on torrents of giggles. I'm thankful for this game and even more thankful that now I get to play it with my son.

Jake Gahr

a simple game

THANK GOD FOR cranberries. Thank bogs
for cranberries. Thank the people who wade into
bogs to harvest cranberries. Thanks for the tart
tang, the teamwork of fruit and sugar, the bright
red berries purpling up as they cook down. Thanks
for the antioxidants. Thanks for the sauce. Thanks
even for canned cran, still in the shape of the can,
wiggling on the table as if it thinks my uncle's jokes
are funny. Thanks for the most vivid flavor on that
table, for making turkey into party food. Thanks,
cranberries. I love you.

Jim Howard

cranberries

discovering

1. **A PUBLIC BATHROOM WHEN I NEED IT MOST.**
2. The trip I didn't want to take that changed my life.
3. That orange candy shaped like big peanuts (no matter what anyone says).
4. When a bird tilts its head and looks at me.
5. The smell of fresh coffee in the morning, especially if made by someone else.
6. The feel of very soft sheets when I'm really tired.
7. The sound of wind ruffling lightly through trees.
8. Discovering a new author I like who's written a whole series of books.
9. S'mores by an open fire.
10. When the home team wins.

Cheryl Hawkinson

A CHALLENGING CROSSWORD

puzzle on a lazy Sunday morning.
Maybe with a Bloody Mary.
A toasted bagel and some
cream cheese would be good, too.
I'm grateful for these simple pleasures.

Rich Pauli

pleasures

I LOVE A good piece of pecan pie. When I see it, smell it, feel its heft on my fork, sink my teeth into its gooey, crunchy, sweet, hearty goodness, I am grateful. Not grateful like, "Oh that's nice." Huh-uh. Grateful from the belly, from the heart of my heart, from my taste buds to my toes. Every bite is a feast, every morsel a celebration of abundance. If you look at it that way (and I do), eating pecan pie is a kind of prayer. Amen to that! And please pass the pie.

Jeannie Hund

ABOUT TEN YEARS AGO, a friend was moving to a city a thousand miles away. Before she left, she planted some moonflower seeds in my garden. What a meaningful gift this has been! Though each moonflower blooms only once, these luminous wonders of nature, their brilliant blossoms popping open on the darkest summer nights, encourage me to embrace optimism and hope in my most troubled times.

Molly Wigand

I'M GRATEFUL FOR challenges, those hard things I never thought I'd make it through but somehow did. I remember once, years ago, loading a moving truck for the fourth time in 14 months and thinking I was saying good-bye to all my dreams, moving backward instead of forward. My feelings of anger, sadness, and failure were nothing close to gratitude. But now I can look back on that and other challenges and see the things I've learned, the way I've been changed, and realize I wouldn't be who I am today without those experiences.

Beverly Laudie

I'M ALWAYS THANKFUL
for my fabulous girlfriends,
who totally get my weirdness.
Melissa Woo

I'M GRATEFUL…

that I don't have to eat liver anymore,

that the last faces I see each night and

the first ones I see every morning are my kids',

that The Rolling Stones keep rockin',

for the color orange on a cold day and

the color blue on a hot day,

for hot sake and cold sesame noodles,

for rainy day puddle splashing.

But mostly, I'm grateful that after all

the years and all the tears, I can still be grateful.

Linda Morris

I RUN. FOR FUN, for exercise. Occasionally, I take on the challenge of a road race, although I'm competing only against the clock and the course. Here's what I've learned about every course I've ever attempted: Sooner or later, I'll come to the downhill part. There's no feeling of gratitude quite like that. Heart, lungs, legs—every participating body part lets go with a rush of relief at the crest of a hill. And then, for a while anyway, I'm faster, stronger, and braver than before. At times in the rest of my life, I keep telling myself it can't be long until the downhill part.

Barbara Loots

CHUNKY PEANUT BUTTER gets my grateful going. There was only smooth when I was a kid. Not that smooth is bad. But chunky is an incredible advance. I just eat it off the spoon. It's the perfect food. A big thanks to whoever put the chunky in peanut butter.

Rich Pauli

I'M CRAZY FOR two-wheeled contraptions—

bicycles, scooters, and motorcycles.

They've given me so much adventure

and some scars along the way.

I cherish every full-throttle acceleration,

45-degree lean, and downhill plummet

that pulls the blood to the back of my brain,

away from the center of reasoning, and sucks

the "yee-haa!" right out of my throat.

John Peterson

adventures

ONE OF MY CO-WORKERS, thankfully, has made it her mission to grace the rest of us with her backyard bouquets. You never know when one of her beautiful arrangements is going to show up on your desk—for no reason at all except as a random act of kindness. But what's even more fun is catching her in the break room as she's snipping stems and filling vases, surrounded by a startling mix of dahlias, marigolds, zinnias, and cosmos. Just seeing that bright burst of creativity and thoughtfulness really perks up my day.

Diana Manning

SWEET MEMORY

I hear a tiny cry through my new-mother dreams.

My husband sleepily shuffles off and returns

with a blanket-wrapped bundle in his arms.

I feed my son, his eyes locked on mine,

and I feel part of a mystery…

How did we all get this lucky?

How can we save this moment in time?

Molly Wigand

WEDDING PICTURES. SEASHELLS.
A jar of Oklahoma red dirt.
Camel statues. Jokes.
Common sense. Armadillos.
Stories. Striped bass. Cowboy boots
and silver belt buckles.

Never older. Never forgotten. Never gone.

Lisa Riggin

MY FATHER STEPPED out of my life when I was a teenager, but I so competently stepped into his place (got a job, paid bills, helped raise my younger brother) that I felt I didn't need a father. I believed that until I married and became the "daughter" of my husband's father. He reminded me of what fathers do. They provide. They provide an ear, support, encouragement, love. My father-in-law is a kind, tender man. We are of different generations, races, faiths, politics. But we are dear friends and treasured family. I love him. I'm thankful for him.

Melvina Young

THIS MORNING, as I relax on the deck with my first cup of coffee, the world feels perfect. Sunshine spreads over fields and pastures. Twelve Canada geese strut beneath my few apple trees, muttering softly. One takes a bite of apple by flinging the rest away with a jerk of its head. Ah, breakfast! I love this time before neighbors awaken. Soon they'll be audible in the distance, adding mower-hum to the music of crickets and songbirds. But for now, the day belongs to the geese and me. And I am awash in thankfulness for this sweet oasis of peace.

Myra Zirkle

RECENTLY, I cleaned out the piano bench and found a note my grandmother had written years ago, my name scrawled on the outside. When I opened it, I found lyrics to one of Grandma's favorite ragtime songs. So many afternoons growing up, I sat next to her on that very bench, watching her play and sing, her voice edged with laughter. As I read the lyrics once more, I smiled, knowing she probably wrote them out for a day like this—when I would relive our moments together. Thank you, Grandma. For the music. For the memories. For singing to me still.

Suzanne Berry

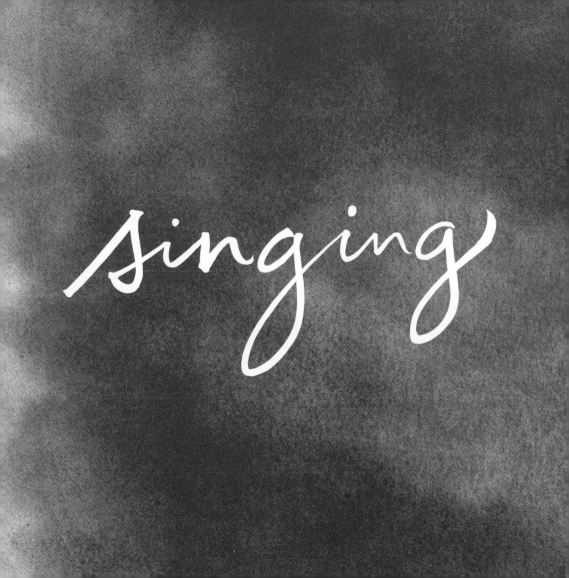

free

AT THIS POINT IN MY LIFE,
I'm grateful for
fat-free anything.

Rich Pauli

YOU KNOW THOSE MORNINGS

when you wake up in a panic
because you think you've overslept
and then it slowly dawns on you,
"This isn't a workday,
it's the WEEKEND—
I can sleep for another eight hours!"
I'm practically teary with gratitude
when that happens.

Dierdra Zollar

Weekends

I'M GRATEFUL FOR

a dolphin's smile, the forgiveness of memory, people who wink, true wit, fresh mozzarella, desire, gumballs, petunias, suspense, twilight, ducklings, money, hummingbirds, kindness, the Marx Brothers, puppy breath, flamingo pink, fitting into my "skinny jeans," whale songs, seeing people happy, fawn spots, Zen koans, people who rescue animals, mystery, air-conditioning, soup bubbling on a stove, the infinite passion of expectation....

Suzanne Heins

A PLUMP, DUSTY,
handpicked blueberry—
juicy, sweet, and happy…very.

Lisa Riggin

I'M THANKFUL FOR my daughter, who reminds me daily what it means to "play." Not with expensive gadgets or mind-numbing computer games, but the kind of "set down the briefcase and get on the floor" play that most work-weary adults have long forgotten. The kind of open childhood play that puts us on our backs in the yard, sky-watching and holding up the clouds with our giggles.

Melvina Young

HERE'S TO THE MISFITS, goofballs, and odd ducks of the world. How dull life would be with everybody thinking inside the same box and no weirdo standing outside it with an idea so crazy it just might work. Here's to the wacky artist, the eccentric inventor, the sidewalk poet, the didgeridoo player in the subway station, the never-a-dull-moment friends who get on our nerves but are absolutely themselves. Here's to questioning authority, refusing to sell out, and wearing funky hats. Thanks for being you, freaks and kooks and crackpots. The world needs you now more than ever.

Jim Howard

I'M GRATEFUL FOR drivers who make way to let me merge from the on-ramp into the main flow of traffic during my rush-hour commute. I'm also grateful when a driver I make way for gives me a little wave of thanks to acknowledge the courtesy—so I do the same for drivers who let me in. These may seem like acts too insignificant to feel gratitude for, but in an age of road rage, I'm thankful for any act that reminds us that there's such a thing as community and that we're all in it together.

Rich Pauli

I'M GRATEFUL FOR my sisters. Because we live in different cities now, I cherish those times when we visit and lie in bed all morning, telling secrets like we did as teenagers. Or walk through the mall together, holding hands the way we used to walk to school together, pausing outside Johnnie's Shop to count how much candy money we had among us. From little girls to women out in the world, we remain as close as ever, as proud of each other as ever.

Kamilah Aisha Moon

compliments

A SWEET FIRST KISS

Having the perfect thing to wear

Compliments

Takeout

Waterproof mascara

Men with sexy accents

French fries

A good sale

Celebrity gossip

Wonderbras

Girlfriends…

those are the things that I'm thankful for.

Melissa Woo

I'M SO THANKFUL I'm not a celebrity, with the tabloids publishing pictures of my fat butt at the beach. I'm thankful, too, I haven't won a huge statewide lottery. With all that money, I'd just nap excessively. (But it might be nice to have a few toadies and sycophants to boss around.) And thank God I haven't won the Nobel Peace Prize. I could never fight with my mother again without her saying, "Oh. So where's the peacemaker now?" I could go on and on about the things I'm thankful not to have. Be thankful I don't.

Suzanne Heins

thankfulness

grandparents

I'M GRATEFUL FOR my grandparents and their old rented hilltop house in Illinois, for the grilled cheese sandwiches smooshed flat in the grill part of their waffle iron, for the grapevines down in the woods behind the house where my cousins and I would swing and yell like Tarzan, for waking to the hum of a long train just past those woods in the middle of the night.

Carolyn Hoppe

I'M THANKFUL FOR advance reservations and RSVPs. If it weren't for them, I'm not sure I'd ever do anything other than work, laundry, cooking, and paying bills. Once I've paid for a ticket, reserved a seat, or promised a child, I'm stuck. I have to go. So I go, and without fail, there'll come a moment when it becomes very clear that going is a very good thing.

Lisa Riggin

simplicity

I AM THANKFUL FOR SIMPLICITY.
A tattered recliner, a well-worn book,
a fragrant cup of plain old coffee
with cream. A telephone ringer that
actually, well, rings. Familiar sheets with
unknown thread counts. Soda crackers
with soup. Great-Aunt Josie's lamp. Things
that let my brain rest and my senses
deepen. Simple things let me just be.
Simple things…fine companions indeed.

Jeannie Hund

I GIVE THANKS FOR basil on vine-ripe tomatoes and bubbly mozzarella. Thanks for nutmeg grated into omelets and sauces. Thanks for cayenne—and its chili pepper kin—for slapping my senses when they're dull. Thanks for rosemary, earthy and aromatic, on pizza and potatoes. Thanks for garlic in everything. Thanks, too, for lowly salt and pepper—wars were fought for them, and I understand why. And a general thanks for all the powders, infusions, leaves, and seeds that tell my taste buds, "Hey, wake up! Time to eat!"

John Peterson

WHAT THIS GIRL'S GRATEFUL FOR...

Strappy sandals,

Twirly skirts,

Fine French wine,

And rich desserts,

New adventures,

Roads untried,

And friends to share

The whole sweet ride!

Diana Manning

I LIKE GOLDFINCHES. Everything about them pleases me, from their petite size to their striking coloring to their nutty, jerky way of flying. I like their cheerful calls and their sociability. I even like their name. No matter how I may be feeling, what I'm doing, or what kind of day I'm having, when I see a goldfinch, I just have to smile.

Rich Pauli

goldfinches

MORE YEARS AGO than I care to acknowledge, as a college freshman, I emerged from the cafeteria after supper into one of those extravagantly glorious sunsets. I gazed into the western sky, enraptured by the blaze of purple and orange and gold. Moments later, friends followed me out the door, and I exclaimed to them, "Look! Just look at that!" "Oh, Barbara," said one of them dismissively. "It does that every day." Yet, even to this day, I try not to neglect being grateful for every beautiful sunset— and every sunrise, too—that I get to see.

Barbara Loots

WEATHER—ALL OF IT—from gentle rain to monsoon, fresh breezes to twisters, hot to frigid—I love it all. I love the power that we can't control, the perfection of a clear blue sky, the never-ending changes that bring about changes in me. I find equal pleasure in the potential that grows within a warm April afternoon and the dormancy that falls over the countryside and my thoughts on a gray December morning. With every passing cloud and breeze, the vision I hold of myself transforms. Keep your fair weather utopia–make mine meteorological!

Lisa Riggin

LOPSIDED HAYRIDES
through ginger-gold leaves,
hot apple cider,
a crisp pumpkin breeze,
homecomings, family,
sweet memories…
How thankful I am for the fall.

Katherine Stano

I AM THANKFUL FOR
waking up to the warmth
of sun shining on my sheets…
birds chirping, a breeze blowing
in the fresh start of a new day.

Melissa Woo

WE'D LOVE TO HEAR FROM YOU
IF YOU HAVE ENJOYED THIS BOOK.

Please send your comments to:
Book Feedback
Mail Drop 215
2501 McGee,
Kansas City, MO 64108
or email us at
booknotes@hallmark.com